BOOK OF KIN

BOOK OF KIN

POEMS BY

DARIUS ATEFAT-PECKHAM

AUTUMN
HOUSE PRESS
PITTSBURGH, PA

Published by Autumn House Press
All Rights Reserved

Book of Kin
Copyright © 2024 by Darius Atefat-Peckham
ISBN: 978-1-637680-96-4

Cover Art: *The Now* by Hemad Javadzade
Book and Cover Design: Melissa Dias-Mandoly
Author Photo: Isabella Farmer

Library of Congress Cataloging-in-Publication Data:

Names: Atefat-Peckham, Darius, author.
Title: Book of kin / poems by Darius Atefat-Peckham.
Other titles: Book of kin (Compilation)
Identifiers: LCCN 2024021063 | ISBN 9781637680964 (paperback) | ISBN
    9781637680971 (epub)
Subjects: BISAC: POETRY / Subjects & Themes / Family | POETRY / Subjects &
    Themes / Death, Grief, Loss | LCGFT: Poetry.
Classification: LCC PS3601.T39 B66 2024 | DDC 811/.6--dc23/eng/20240508
LC record available at https://lccn.loc.gov/2024021063

Printed in the United States on acid-free paper that meets the international stan-
dards of permanent books intended for purchase by libraries.

Autumn House Press is a nonprofit corporation whose mission is the publication
and promotion of poetry and other fine literature. The press gratefully acknowledges
support from individual donors, public and private foundations, and government
agencies. This book was supported, in part, by the Greater Pittsburgh Arts Council
and the Pennsylvania Council on the Arts, a state agency funded by the Common-
wealth of Pennsylvania.

TABLE OF CONTENTS

THE FIRST SOUND

BOOK OF KIN

THE OUTER REACHES

for my family

Then praise the wordless speaker I am.
I raced through emptiness, footless like the moon.
Praise the footless runner I am!

Rumi

THE FIRST SOUND

WIND CHIMES

The first sound was the ax blade
shucking away

my bones. Toes muffled
in shields of plaster. It's been years.

Once he prayed
his hair to hand dryers at the Y

his hand
                 a comb, or a shower

readying him
for the day. We were the same

age, then. How can I begin
to make sense of this? The smell, old

vomit steeping years
in the passenger seat. The dog dazing, my fingers

traveling the warmth of its large
maw. Dad, our pilot, munching at 3 a.m.

on a breakfast burrito, steering our car
through an intersection

with his knees. I used to tell him
everything. My wish

                            alive again

that I could hear my mother

        sadaya khesh khesh

as radio static, the shuffle of feet
kissing leaves, to this day

I have no idea

what it sounds like. Only intimations of
a woman for whom

I'd draw rivers back
into their valleys, my father undoing

like laces: your mother's laugh [khesh]
was like a—Bear—Honey,

it was like something—

the fullness of time—full of
[hush] music. This final

[sadaya]

sound. *Like that?*

[   ]

THE TURKISH COFFEE LADY

Tysons Corner Center, Tysons, VA

I have this issue: I am too many sons to too many mothers.
I approached you at your shop, inherited from your Persian mother.

When I was a boy, I blurred my vision, gave the dark-haired boys
my story, mothers at the periphery. Everywhere they turn: mothers

and not-mothers. Forgive me. When I summoned you, you were
already another shade of mother. I thought of Afghan mothers

in train cars, singing one to another. I have disgraced my own
mother's death time and again with mystery, blasphemy, Mother

Earth and her offspring. I made sense of it. I speak to you like I'm still
your son, you my mothers. I offer a place mat, a chair, christen you *mādaram*

as you teach me to address myself. *Darrish, Darroosh, Daryoos.* I shush
your eyes. Lead you in prayer. I feel galaxies. I wish upon my own mother:

visit me just once. Meet me, sitting there, across the table, so we can swirl
our pinkies in the grounds. Look at me: these eyes that fill the empty air,

this face that opens easily, like a flower, like a boy calling after
a skinned knee in so many languages, mouth warm and worn with *Mother.*

My hand breaks a piece of halva. The Turkish Coffee Lady calls *Dariush.*
I rise to set down my steaming cup. Smiling, I pay my Persian mother.

IN A CHILD'S HAND

The first thing that died by my hands
was a hermit crab. The cosmos

was painted clumsily across
the canvas of its back.

It relied on me

and I forgot it
for weeks, living

in the same room, breathing,
myself. The saddest thing

I ever saw, all those legs,
its shell, kicked aside

like a blanket too hot
for the night.

~

My body

across a highway, paling
in the sun, retching

my entire life across the grass, into
a forest I might never

return to. My father,

his big arms crossed. *If you love your grandparents
so much why don't you go live*

with them. My grandparents,

aging. *If you love your father so much
why do you bother*

coming to visit. Many times, I close
my eyes, ask

for my mother, and receive
what I think to be

                                        just a sound

around me.

~

I used to cry so hard I wanted to hide
what came from me,

a breaking, an accumulation
the way moons are formed, a link

to the earth, the sea. A mother
who will never leave, never die,

who will die, many times, over
and over, but stay
                                        there

on that shore, ready
to receive me. To gather, make a nest of me

in a child's hand, send me

                                reeling

back again.

THE BIRTHDAY FAIRY

I never believed in you. But your calling
pinned my eyes shut. Radiance followed
the murmured question of my name. *Darius?*
You awake? Lustering planets, awkward
gentle flight of them like anything new
and sown. I held the balloons to my eye
like stained glass and looked in at the light.
There seemed to be millions; I counted
to stay awake. I believed we invented
everything. Tradition. My mother. All that joy

carried from a time before. Dad grinning in
the doorway. *Looks like the Birthday Fairy*
made you a visit. Even then, I knew belief
was just a story I told myself. Only tasting it,
like a kiss, to be sure. Can you believe
I thought you were my father? Who sat
in the living room most nights, weeping into
his hands. Who moaned the night
from his room. My eyes sewn shut, peeking
through the dark of my mother's long lashes.
Whose breath lives inside me? Whose light
hooks through the face of me now?

SUNDERED SONNET: IF WE SHOULD BE GHOSTS

Scrape / of boys flipping heel-kicks off a stoney face. Creak of widows casting flowers in the dirt. Crush of the couple in my dreams tasting each other beneath the whitening sycamore. My heart stops each time I think of losing someone / I actually remember. Little reason to delay my everyday / haunts. I laminate my laments, frightening them short of love / poems. After sleepovers, my classmates whisper their findings. *They live / in a Haunted House.* Who had they heard? Dad, crying *Welcome to the family!* each time a guest stumbled in on any embarrassing thing. Sopping the years in his apron for the sake of cake. Cautioning, there's only enough / for nobody, as the rental crumbles into ruin around us. I'd like some savings, so I can have a little ghoul of my own one day. Not a spirit or saint. Or, ghost / help me, a child. I've wanted grief so long, growing it / like a gesture, grooming it like a pig for the fair. Looking like me. Haunted / by playgrounds. Ghosted by crushes. Happening upon the sound / of my crying cowering like a child up too late and hiding within my ear, eerily familiar. I'm a ghost / fearing man. I go to the graveyard every birthday eve, calling. I break / like the fog gathering on a boy's glasses. I pay my respects steady as the night mists that come each dawn watering / the stones.

THE PATIENT STONE

She wants to send the letter of her body
home. *Nastaliq shekasteh*. Broken handwriting.

She wants to join the protests, burn
her hijab. I would forbid it if I could: her

leaving me. I wish to be the patient stone.
The patient stone listens. Absorbs

the sorrows of those who confide in it.
When two beings are inseparable, *and*

is pronounced *o*. Layla o Majnun,
gol o morg, Khosrow o Shirin, my Bibi

o her country. Séance of my ear harboring
secrets, dribbling like a mouth

at a fountain. Our voices cling to one another.
Our eyes distend, bursting. As I wait

to board my train, she asks how
my Persian is *doing* as if it is a sick relative

or a child in trouble at school. The man in me
grovels his sorrows in the desert basin,

his memory making mud from the dirt.
*Even I—Even I—Even I—*I say. She listens.

DAR HAVĀYAT, IN YOUR AIR

When I was born, I had a thick head full
of *beautiful Iranian hair.* How frustrating

to have what you want inside
outside. In 2020, in 1398, the Islamic Republic

shoots an airplane filled with its own citizens
out of the sky. When I tell

a grad student at a party, he says to the guy
by the fridge, *King Daroosh, here, needs*

a drink. I can feel his breathing
creep down my neck and into

my shirt. I've never felt comfortable
in graveyards. Sitting at kitchen tables,

Bibi tells me my mind will soon
close up, close out: a bird flown

into a porch screen or a balloon tied off
for a child, for me. I was unbearably happy

at carnivals, thinking of nothing
at all. I ate too much and threw up

behind Ferris wheels, felt the sting of
the air filling me up. I worried after

what they taught me. After ghosts and spirits and if
they really existed. Everywhere I went I opened

my mouth in apology, made space for them
and wondered if they made space

in me. The sheer number, the magnitude
of their unearthly forms, how

we must walk through them. When my Bibi thinks
I've done something well, she says *You are*

doing amazingly good! In her English,
the good I've done is

staggering. Overflowing. Enfolding
and encircling. Mothering me

away from my air. How
is it that I am without

wings?

MOTHER

No matter how still I become, I am still
spinning. I see my self in

every thing. Crawling, yawning,
swimming, digging. Knowing

I have a before, only
after. I have learned this much: the lake

is a mother. I am feathered, buoyant in
its swell. If you long for time

enough, absence becomes
a kind of presence. Distance taut as a line

between us. No cord is broken.
My ears carry this beating

heart like a breath.

SECOND MOTHER

for Rachie

In dream, dreaming,
I am not terrified
of my death, but

of yours. How selfish.
Persians take special interest
in dreams. In dreams

my professor presses Farsi
into my mouth like gol,
refusing to take soil. It is not

prophecy, but everything
below. I have risen from
that kind of sleep

to no one. From the tub
as a boy, I'd swoon
then collapse. If my father

hadn't heard the soft body
hit, I'd rise from
the linoleum. Shaky,

alone. And run
to you. Excited, almost
for your concern. To be

embraced and
alive. In the holding
pattern of one's

stoppered breathing, I
name you. Mothers.
How selfish.

What we secrete in
these bodies is
not called weeping.

THE HOUSE WHERE I WAS BORN

for Isabella

Where I watch you pull on and peel off my
grandmother's clothes. She works late into the night

mending these fabrics for you. She asks after your weight,
your dimensions, leads you by the arm as if into the meadows

of many closets filled with all I've failed to inhabit—body-
suits, evening gowns, belts and buckles and shoulder pads.

I only stop my Bibi at her casual mention of the wedding
dress, my mother's, her wink like one of many pearls

painstakingly inlaid by her own hand. I watch as you play
dress-up, become my mother, my grandmother—moments

you even become yourself. Now you laugh and twirl
on garden stones in Tehran. Now you step across boardwalks

in Geneva, smile back. In the village-town of Kalpurgan,
they believe that earth is medicinal. They paint clay into each other's

bodies. It cured. They wash themselves clean. Something goes
as they watch bits of themselves become the river. Something

stays. Here and together, I touch you, selfish, hungry, barely
checking over my shoulder the way I always do, your chilled palm

pressing my face into your shoulder, playing a bit with the small
hairs of my neck. Unpainted, earthen. The house

creaks. Someone pauses, ascending the stairs. Listening. Dust
plumes off the duvet. *It's been so long since someone's*

actually lived here, I tell you. We stop and start again, afraid,
laughing like kids practice-kissing in the dark.

ONCE MOURNED

Tell no one about the ghosts
fluttering up against glass
as you wait in line for security.

Your mother once
snuck her pet gerbil through
like a fugitive tucked in the barrel

of a toilet paper roll. All that,
just so the secret body
could die in the strong maw

of her husband's boyhood
dog. The natural order
of things. What the crow does

on the side of the hot dirt road
is a kindness. To untie a body
from itself, a kindness,

though a story
always comes knocking
to be let back in its shell.

Your mother once mourned.
You can never quite depart.
A woman just ahead of you

says to her child,
over and over:
I'm not disappearing.

THEY WAKE ME

Car alarms bleating along an empty block.
How many beloveds in me will I survive?

Sour as berries that died on the vine. My fingers stay
In the mouth of astonishment. Can such a shell survive?

Even Forugh must have run her hands to water.
Pendulum heads foretell how few survive.

Like the owl of Sunday morning cartoons, I want
To see what, at the tongue of a cracked bell, survives.

A citizen of my catchall drawer. A keepsake of
The stayed-behind. A one-way ticket, that will to survive.

I reach time. I step in front of a honking car—jump
Back. I outlive myself. Can't help but survive.

Veiled mother flickers bodily in the lamplight
Of you. Steps, unsteps in the melt that survives.

Yours was more than a death. Must mine be more than
A life? In your orbit, that unending scrawl: *She is survived* . . .

I spell my name with each footfall in dirt. Always
Incorrect. I reach palms down that wet well. Survive.

DEATH REPORT

1.

The first visitation
                                    is a dream, I lift

my eye to her
like my living is a prison. I tell

the time by how hot
my tongue became. Her face

a hazy glimpse of moon—far, far.
Her gaze rushes through

the bars.

2.

My father calls
the voice droning
                                    above, *Death*

Report. My eyes stay cold, tucked in
their beds. Their names, pronounced,

no matter what I do. The eyes
of my American parents

bore into their American son. *They
aren't kind*
                    to our citizens

there. My self
unfurls, steady for the bell.

All this practice, and still
my mouth stumbles like a man carrying

his son from the car. What if
it were *my* name in

the Death Report. Would I still
my mouth. Lie cold in my cell.

Would the need to linger die
with me, away.

3.

Once, on our way
home from a funeral, I played

dead in the car. I wanted my father's breath
to catch. I wanted to be still

and have him
                          hold me. He rolled

his eyes. *Seriously?*
His breath, smooth

and current. My head against
his chest. Sleep is not

Death, Mother, forgive me
my perennial living. I doze off

whole. Let someone carry me
the rest of the way home.

I LEARN A LANGUAGE I'M TOO AFRAID TO SPEAK

Sometimes I pretend it's just a matter
of stones. It isn't the entire world
there, beside me. I'm not the boy
who received it, nails ravaged by
the pickax of his mouth. Bibi, gifting me
this paperweight globe the size of
her heart. The most precious stones
in history have been
plundered. Stolen. Gifted
and broken apart. I can't help
what it is, what we are, my father
raising a brow at this unnecessary tether
my grandmother hands me, the small
gold pendant I wear around
my neck, even now, for the rest of
my life. My entire family in Iran
pitched in, she tells me.
The aunt I've spoken to
just once this year
chose it. Fashioned after
the king I'm named for.
Or kings—one revered, one
murdered. One about which little
is known. *A gift with strings
is not a gift at all,* my father can't help
but say. All my strings shudder
at the sound like some black sail
in this sprawling sea.

ALL BODIES

As in every language,
there are different words
for all bodies

of water. Somehow
it still surprises me
how many. Like the goldfish

who died one after
another in the days leading up
to *Nowruz*, the *New Year*

whispering
at their budding
lips. There are rules:

I don't know them yet.
From what I can tell,
rudkhaneh is *House*

of River. The *Ocean*
encompasses
the *seas*. You will find

fountains and *springs*
in any suburban
yard, boys' hands

submerged within them.
Once kayaking,
my small boat

turns turtle
in the rapids. Like a fish,
I am betrayed

by my own open
mouth. For fourteen days,
I drown in my

great-grandma's kitchen,
and the *sabzeh* grows
backward into

itself. The rings
of my scales sound
outward. My belly

splits open
the surface. I
die like this, watching

the people twirl together
like water bugs, their
empty, laughing *mouths*

of *rivers, Oases*
holding the *Rain* easily
as upturned boats.

IF I WANT TO GO THERE I HAVE TO WATCH WHAT I SAY

Today, jogging, I tell my father *ask me anything*
and I'll give it back. He watches his step, says look
out for snakes after rain. Some people here
carry knives to sever them at the head. I give
the word for snake instead of knife or rain. *mār*
I say in Farsi like a cat. The royal librarian
of Golestan Palace is imprisoned for stealing
manuscripts. He is guilty, is ailing, is dying soon
after he is freed. Cartloads of first editions
wheel back through the city. My father again

names the wrong flower that opens with
the rain. Laughing, he remembers their politeness—
taarof—so intense they could hardly get out
the door, the house, repeating *You go first, no*
you as if they'd forgotten how to begin. He begins,
informal, impolite: *Really you should be able to*
go to Iran, really you should have no trouble
at all. Awaiting a sentence, a sculptor stands
up high in a tiny apartment, teeth yellowing
as he smiles. If I want to go there, I must learn

to speak on my own behalf. *zandān*, I say,
prisoner. I move my lips carefully around
the sounds to get them right, a quiet
breaststroke. *zendegān*, the living, leafing
through dictionaries. In Farsi, I fear naming
incorrectly or not at all. *Once*, my father smiles,
in a plane on her way home my mother deleted
an entire poem. Maybe it's trouble
that I want. I want to wear a beard, to rush
through a park, a square, an absence

of statues, with papers so essential they're clutched
to my hand. Maybe by writing this I'm losing
all hope. Khaleh Nina screams out in the garden.
In a Tehran hospital. The red crescents of her eyes
look up, finally, to greet me. *Here's the thing—*
my father, striding, lays it out like a daily ration;
he is unreasonable, irrational—what's the word
for this? I tell him I want to be covered,
clothed in the darkness of night. Reach out
to drooping branches and plumb their greening.
Treat my gardens like libraries, pick flowers with

no intentions of bringing them back. In practice-
Persian, I get my father's phrases half-right.
I detain myself in everything I name
beautiful, and say nothing. A copper snake appears
on the path like a heat wave ahead of us. Its mouth
opens, watching to make sure we pass. My father's breath
quickens. He mutters, *Pick up the pace.* My heart
racing. I want to stop and stare. I want to reach out
my hand. I don't want any of this at all. *Hurry,*
he says. *Befarmāyid, Welcome, Here you are, Please, No you.*

ACTIONS, PRESENCES, SCARS

But what if ghosts aren't perpetual
in dying? Rather, singing. Old bone
creaked forward listening
to the summer vegetable shook
loose from its soil. Like the upset dirt,
most prefer the word *spirit*. Free, untethered.
Who would want something like that?
Scare me a little. Make me a bit
afraid of what accompanies me. What Dad called
good fear when I ran to him after a bad fall,
knowing it might have ended me. I am good
afraid of ghosts. Their cool fingers conjuring my brow.
Their dirge-like mourning for the dead in us.

POST-LOSS CHECKLIST

1.

Have I done all I'm
supposed to? I wear clean
socks. I wash
my hands and try
to pray. *khak bar saram.* I say
I should die, I should have
dirt on my head. I wear a slight
smile. I sit high up
in the breeze. I become
small again, tapping my fingers
along empty clotheslines.
Along headstones
to wake the dead. They hear
me. They yawn
and stretch like trees.

2.

Have I done all I'm
supposed to? The cardinals
visit today. I try to make
them laugh by telling
the joke I can't
remember. Their beaks
open and close
like sighing. I ask
if there are rules to this. *God,*
they answer out from
my mouth. *And he is here,*
they say, knocking loudly
on their small skulls.

3.

I had my first dreaming
a while back. We sat together
in a car and spoke of all
I can't remember. When
I look at you, my smile
wavers, looks a-grimace. I have
no idea who I am trying
to be. But I think you know
I don't make a good mouth-
piece. I grow my hair, I wear
my clothes and stay
clean. Just another
gentle curve of body, just
another funny face. And I think
I remember now:

4.

I have gone. They are
supposed to be taking me
back like a sculptor
to an unfinished
stone. Say *dooset daram*,
I love you. *khodahafez*,
goodbye. I am going
to the gravesites. In the winter
months, when the flowers
are frostbit and dying, I go
like this: one hand
tapping the stone, one hand above
my head, pouring the earth.

HEATHCLIFFS

The face of a moon peaks
from beneath Isabella's shirtsleeve.
She holds her dress at either side like wings.
Is it raining there? Is there mud? Born
from the soil, dusted clean, put to
my lips. I plan to have many. They will know
who I am, accrued across my fingers, hung
down hollows of my neck, waiting to be lost
back. How do I mean? I am not meant
for this. I stand in the rain, dumbfounded and
searching, wiping myself from my eyes. I wait
for the right conditions to put my self
to practice. I wear a new ring for every day
of my life. I am told to express myself
this way, just nothing permanent, *please.*
I am obsessed with myself. Like a planet,
I long for something I can't slip off at night
and forget to wear in the morning. I want
to make it all wuthering, whatever
that means. I want to be clothed, fed, taken
care of. The hands of my love. The accidental
salt of fingertips, an ocean at my lips, teaching me
something about worship. That question
there, sealing me shut: if she was too good
for this world, as they say, what does that
make me, still standing here, gathering
myself at the gate?

CYRUS

The first sound was the quieting
of my fingers brushing
the first, brief shocks of hair
from your head. Still. There

when our father said
we had five seconds to cry
before he'd get angry
or cry himself. When the child psychiatrist

watched you play
with ghosts, diagnosed
seems like a perfectly happy
child to me. Am I

both or neither of us
now? My fingers through your hair
aren't so much fingers
anymore. Not so much touch. Absence

you'll bear now for the rest
of our lives. Half-drowned
tree in a lake shrouded
in mist. Your forehead

like a steaming cup
to my lips. Brother,
there are many
different ways to sing yourself

to sleep. *Like in your head?*
Our father asked. *No,* our mother
mouthed. *Like I'm speaking*
to you now.

BOOK OF KIN

PORTHOLE

for opening eyes to the salt
of the earth, see: the ocean: see: watching
home movies so old they no longer play: for so
old, see: *kaash*: for *kaash,* see: wish: see: their endings:
for endings, see: boy at the top of the stairs: see: mother
pointing ethereal lens: for spoilers, see: their endings,
ending no different from yours: for yours, see: wan-
dering about the silent space: for space, see:
shutting the eye of the mind: see: re-
membrance like bits of sea
currency run ashore

BOOK OF KIN

"people are calling god with all their heart. maybe their voices will shake the kingdom of god . . ."

He is the living & dead. He navigates

    [America] by starlight beneath bridges

over diverted rivers, knotting His carpet's

    tassels into magic figure eights. He learns

to [will] bits & pieces of us from

    His dreams. The Boy-Seeking kisses

the archive of our breath. this is how

    He learns to breathe. words rising

in bubbles of air we hold in our shells, our selves

    cracking & breaking apart. can He [do

what is necessary]? love anyone who

    [states] their denial plain, wears a cape

only to remove it: [like these] magicians

    [and] matadors, sufis in [their] white burial

dresses & tall tombstone hats, [terrorist]

in her hijab offering flowers to soldiers

to prevent them from shooting. guns empty

as watering cans reaching toward

her. [allies], [constitute] His secret muraled

faces, [an axis] of samaras, whirligigs, wing tips

weaving in & out [of] this [evil] body [arming

to threaten] His time below. mother,

life-giver, water who must return. you

who makes [the peace of] our name.

to be left like this. it takes [the world]. make Him

unsurprised by those who remain.

PORTHOLE

for man, see: king: see: *farr*: see:
seeking: for seeking, see: boy: see: boy-
king: for human, see: *adam*: see: *saadi*: see:
tree: for tree, see: country, see: *keshvar*: see: *khak*:
see: soil: for sea, see: *darya*: see: body: see: writing: for
writing, see haunt: see: *didar makrar kardan*: see:
frequent visits: see: dreaming: for dream, see:
waking: see: involuntary listening: for
listening, see: to see, again &
again: in persian, 'i' is *man*

BOOK OF SLEEP

*"many of us don't even believe in god, but each night we come and on god we call for
the others, for those who died, for me, for you, for Iran. the voices are coming from
far away. they leave you shaken. . . . I wonder if god is shaking too."*

The Boy-Seeking will never understand

       how His father reads

by osmosis. each night, falling asleep,

       one ear open, [steadfast] as a plant

drawing breath, eating darkness.

       each morning, rising, eyes

straining through a new light, turning

       to dust. is it possible to listen [in]

a new language? The Boy-Seeking has before

       fallen asleep only to be woken

with a start, [our] memories rearranging

       the bones of His ear like a boxer's after

a bout. all of a sudden struck, all of a sudden

      the [purpose] of life prodding

the hard softness of his scalp. is it possible to be

      changed, just like that? is there

such thing as successful revolution? to awaken

      His father's fear that his boy, seeking,

might never find home. that He'll find

      home, but home won't be

with him. how to reconcile the [we]

      & [now]? to learn one, must He lose

the other? another thing He'll never

      understand: how to write that word

they called Him. how to forgive

      His own tongue. for years, He'll erase &

[press] space for pause. He'll plummet

      down deep ocean canyons, looking through

eyes that aren't His own & back

    to His father, awake, hand resting on

His spine, saying *shhh* & *I don't want you to be*

    haunted for the rest of your

life. maybe we do become

    what we're called [on] to be. or maybe

it's just too painful, the alternative,

    that His father never sleeps.

PORTHOLE

for your first mistake, see: you
can't learn any language by speaking: for
any language, see: *zaban*: see: deep listening:
see: your mother's kitchen table: for cooking, see:
dorost kardan: see: to make: see: her hands making
words deep inside her boy's mouth: for mouth,
see: ear: for ear, see: eye: for eye, see: aye, aye
captain!: for 'i,' see: 'you': for 'i,' see:
should i   live? or   or

". . . defenseless people who have been called 'dirt and dust,' defenseless people who have expressed themselves with silent and peaceful protest, now at night from the kingdom of god ask for help."

[our enemies] at the ninth-grade lunch table

      plot to confuse & muddle, to dredge

what is lost in the seas between countries. calling Him

      "bomb," calling Him "terrorist," calling

Him "dirty muslim sand-[   ]."

      The Boy-Seeking will spend His entire

life filing onto football fields in His jordans,

      snaking through securities before He ever learns

to [send] His body home. He'll notice how

      [other people's children] walk

differently, as if through different spaces. He mounts

      a stony steed. rides into caution

like a boy bloodied from the garden, [on] imaginary

      [missions], sneaking past that marble [of] mother

on the porch swing, invisible, hands daring prayer

            as she waits for Him to arrive home

from His war, His slow [suicide]. for Him to shout

            her name, to fall to hands [and] knees like a man

at a [murder]. to avoid this, [we choose] Him

            a rug. we advise He hang it on the wall,

a tapestry. He looks at us, sleepless as a newborn

            father. on the wall, He can't sink

His knees in its canopy & pretend

            He's reached [freedom]. on the wall,

it's like a porthole, borderless, His hands

            rubbing stars in the slick, hundreds of

years of untouched window He sees

            through. [and] His own likeness

there, appearing in [the] mirror of its half-

            silk face. o tiny nebulas of dust. o little [dignity

of] His mouth, dry as [every] river. when

He dies, this land He's carried will re-

surface. after He's lived a long & happy

[life], The Boy-Seeking will return.

PORTHOLE

for life, see: splintered
windows in a ship-wracked
vessel: for vessel, see: *keshti*: see: grand-
father's Mercedes: see: its leather-lined seats
& cardboard diaper in the garage: see, *my car, it's still
running great!*: for run, see: *bodo, bodo!*: for grandfather, see:
bozorg: see: papa: watching numbers soar & sink, stock-
still in the a.m. & when he's lost enough, the numbers
turn to scripture & his eyes open shut & letters
leak peaceful as oil across the black-
screened sea: for sea, see: shaken:
for shaken, see: *didan*: see: to
insight & incite: for
site, see: kin

THE OUTER REACHES

THROAT OF YOUR HOUR

after The Now *by Hemad Javadzade*

Deep-sea diver. Mystic
astronaut pondering
pestle of chin
in your palm—stars
plunking against the hollow
of your helmet. You need
a moat. You think to
yourself. Cyclops eye. Ghost
king. Your subjects
numberless as
the night's pulse. Place
the mirror of your seeing
to its yawning. Newborn
Reaper. Gaze crawling
up the throat of
your hour. Holy
geometer. Wise soul. Old
boy. Stay—you know
the word for it—alive.

THE OUTER REACHES

BAHRAM ATEFAT   SUSAN ATEFAT-PECKHAM
                                         1970 – 2004

FARIDEH BARATI-ATEFAT   CYRUS ATEFAT-PECKHAM
                                         1997 – 2004

All of a sudden, I am the only one living.

Peering into the silence of yet another text.

Drifting in the outer reaches. Their names,

like tenants of the flood, wading in

nearness. She takes the watering can,

leaving me with prophecy, just a bit of rust

in the lines of my palm. Surprising me, she steps

past the eager soil and breathing flowers,

lets her grief tumble down the granite

shoulders, (how she used to clean my back

when I could hardly stand, *Time*—she'd sing

sloughing the rough washrag against my nape. Sand

to stone and oh, how I'd crow at the tickle

and hurt of her love, never turning to see her face)

washing the mum stone of pollen and dust.

THE NIGHT BEFORE MY MOTHER DIED, THEY SLEPT IN SEPARATE ROOMS

Someone's tongue
crests. I am constantly
knowing more

than I wish to know.
If my father
were not my father,

I'd tell him
about the last time
I saw my mother.

In the hospital
the morning after
she died. I think

it was morning.
I woke to blinding light
and my crying

and my crying
was my first memory.
This woman. Her jeweled

hand. The white-
coats bustling
through.

HAUNT

for Tāhirih—poet, activist, martyr

When the Eyes open, finally,

they won't yield

to touch. Like ice-

flowers reaching to catch the soil. To blossom,

the mystics wrote, is to open

her smile. A man sits, head

wrapped, holding conversation

with a parking meter. A real poet haunts, her mouth

full of white silk, singing quiet

to take *our* breath away. *Tā*

meaning: so that, up to, until

then, rather than—sometimes, even,

when. Is translation the least

we can offer? What remains

down the well that terrifies us

so, that we offer pebble

and coin to bury it. Some men learn

to be ghosts before they ever

learn to die.

SURROUNDINGS

"Isfahan's Friday Prayer Imam, Yousef Tabatabei-Nejad ... once again urged Iran's security and intelligence agents to make the 'surroundings unsafe' for citizens with a 'loose hijab.'"

Radio Farda, October 4, 2020

Sing a man's poem again. Your beard is nothing
But a bad hijab failing to hide your face.

      Would a hijab hide a smoldering face?
      Your Bibi dyes a bad hijab, her fingers in her hair.

Says, *not too bad*, the hijab. Fingers back her dying hair.
You are her only son, so you are like the moon.

      You are only her grandson, so she is the moon—
      The "spectacle" her father punished for singing.

Remember Father, in his spectacles. Remember her singing.
She was a songbird, combing through hair, building her nest.

      You are a songbird, stealing hair to build your nest.
      Your Bibi won't sing anymore. You'll never hear her

Sing over your apology. You'll never hear her
Sing a man's poem again. Your beard is nothing.

LEARNING TO PRAY

Practicing yoga with my second mother,
my father maneuvers, splits his hip bone
like roots, the Yogi on-screen sings, *unfurling
into the ground.* I think of my great-grandfather,
my first mother—a young girl—watching him
from beyond the doorway as he prays
his body in shapes and forms toward God,
his mustache brushing the ground, and I
wonder whether my grandparents are *real*
Muslims, real Iranians, real parents. I could ask,
though I've never found them bent to Mecca
or to anything—Bibi, halving fruit, saying
she doesn't need some compass to show her
which direction faces home; my mother
and brother are every direction and no direction
at once. She asks me if I understood. *You
understood?* And the world slows. And I am
the old man who often thrusts his furious
head through the shutter of my face. My chin
tilts heavy on my chest, my body whirling
without ever leaving my mat. I listen for it.
The earth's warning, how close it is to
rain. My father, my brother and mother, my
second mother. Even this, a tiny spider
balancing on a hair on my arm. The roots of
its little legs, trying to make a home there.

HERE'S A LOVE POEM SLEEPING

together in bed, thinking how much
I love your tired voice, *tired you*

I call it, love

                    the tired

curve of your back, your tired
breathing, love it when you roll your *r*'s and scrunch

your nose, speak the ghost
of your Spanish better

than the Persian I'm trying to learn
now. How sometimes, all these years

later, you ask if I'm mad
that you're sleeping. You're doing it

again now, faced toward me, eyes
worried and awake: *are you mad at me*

for sleeping? I am thinking

                    of my family

in Iran. They call you my fiancée, a smirk
in their voices as I search for something

they may understand: *khoshgelam, zendegiam, moosham,*
ham-dam—my beautiful, my life, my mouse, my

same breath. My Bibi telling me
which photos to send

to my ammeh on her WhatsApp. *Do you have any*
without her shoulders? Without her stomach? Without her

legs? I search for a picture of you without
your body. *She looks even a bit Iranian*

in her face. You, laughing, asking if you have a face

like the moon. My Bibi laughing

at wedding bells, exclaiming, *Another*
donkey joins the show! Sometimes I wish I could

shelve my memories, climb into the smell
of that principal's office in the cold, pinch

my eyes shut—five seconds, ten, twenty—then
open, thinking

like a magic trick, of

you, that you might stride through
those heavy school doors to

pick me up, spin me round, set me down
again. My father, crashing

through, alone, a donkey, jaw clenched—
the cop who stopped him for swerving, asked him

to walk in a straight line. He couldn't. The lights
of oncoming traffic crashing into his faltering

back, the cop holding his flashlight like
a gun against his shoulder. *Listen,*

buddy, we can do this

        all day. How he measured

the distance of longing. Ancient
Persian astronomers measured the stars

with a device called the star-taker. Measured
bodies bent to their instruments. My father's

        first bad marriage. What

I came from. Hands. Stars

all around. The school-secretary, looking at
us, with a little pity, less

understanding, as we limped away from her
into the dark. Your face toward

me, bodiless and shining. *I don't want to sleep
if you're not sleeping, too.* I close

my eyes to you like a man splashing
bits of the river against

        his face.

OF BLUEBERRIES

Just minutes before
       the anniversary, I am
    inexplicably thinking

of blueberries, and
       the slowness of my love
    crushing some

with her teeth. *Golrokh*
       is flower-faced, lacking
    equivalence. I've seen many

things I haven't seen. Like a man
       sanitizing his utensils
    methodically with an onion

on Pahlavi Avenue.
       Like the swift bursting
    of many fruits. Under

ideal conditions, a blueberry bush
       lives sixty years. The way
    my mother lived, maybe,

half the life of a blueberry
       bush, crown jewel of
    Iran, first masterpiece

of god, eyes, dark
       sheen before ruin. In Persian,
    there's no good word

for blueberry. In the soil
       there, this fruit, its too much
    life, is made nearly

impossible. And so I go
   seeking in the silence between
  my beloved's teeth, and

as I see it, these moments, are
   myth. Eyes. Little blue
  wounds of flesh

risen like night. It is
   just comfort and I
  am just thinking. I am always

thinking. There is only
   so much life
  to live. Only so much time

under ideal conditions.
   So much. Only so much.

IMAGINE THE LAKE. CYRUS IS ALIVE

and dancing about with stones
in his pockets, checking behind. All kid
brothers do. He trudges

into the lake. A fisherman on the rocks
letting wave after wave
get his socks wet. The water

reaches his chin. His Buzz Lightyear
tennis shoes sink into the mud
of Lake Michigan. He wades there. There

is a woman overlooking the water: Bibi,
clearer now, on a bench, just thinking
for—imagine it—*hours*. We

are behind her, arriving home
from a long walk down
the lakeshore. Shaking our heads. *She's*

waited, we say, *all this time?* We look
away. We are talking
of escape. The planetarium. A version

of ourselves who may have thought,
how big, the universe. Existence beyond
this array of planets and stars

as real as the earth. Some great
shell. The turtles beneath us as we swim
the translucent sea, coming up

for air. *Turtle!* we cry
as they disappear.
Turtle! Turtle! as they appear,

again. We shout, even
when—over and over—we are
unsure. Specular. Peering

in—through—the water.

CORONATION

Covering the boy's eyes, I whisper, *You*
              are your father's

father. Eye of his feathered throne. Your mouth,
receiving his ghosts

like a bit of milk

clung to your lip. Wipe it, bitter
as a tear, away. Turn north

from the woman, her mind beaten naked in a van.
From the child, his thoughts blooming through

his shirt. Your second thought is

always true. Take it, and forgive
yourself. Lead

a comatose state. No matter, no mothers

in you. The crown is a pink mouth worth biting.
You are your own

son. North is north, wherever

you are. Directionless. Silent:
this space of *as if*
                    to say, it is

fathers all the way down.

SUNDERED SONNET: THEY SAY I SPEAK BETTER PERSIAN THAN

my mother, but she was a crow, soaring across landmarks I know / singing *moosh bokhoradet!* Fluent in phrases of the mother tongue. Wasn't she? *You look so much like your mother. We are so proud of you.* Taarof is extreme politeness, a lovely / way of lying. Cigarette ashes falling like leaves in the drain of my mind. I look at the last surviving / sister on WhatsApp, upside-down and muted. I run out / of words. I laugh, I correct myself. The closest I come to time / travel is when they say *you already have, in your mama's belly.* Like a well-loved stuffy tied to the grill of a truck, traveling across highways. Trying to be / a talisman, quieting bored ghosts up to no good. *inshā'Allah, inshā'Allah,* forever *inshā'Allah.* I just need to be immersed. A shipwreck. To rack / my memory for the sights, the taste of sky in her belly, holding her sleeve as we wander that home together. Lantern of her / hand, pointing here or there a king's burial place, his limestone womb, umbilical shuddering / the wind. Lovelier than / I mean to. I want to be the only child of grief. I want the swears and curses of the mother tongue, her soul sat on my lips. Their silence. The closest I come / to stillness. My mother scolding me, waving a correcting hand, brushing the hair from / my eyes.

MEMORIAL MURAL FOR THE PERSIAN [PICASSO]

Begin at the farm where sullen cows are pimped out seventy-five dollars a hug to the lonely people

Where I wish to be now hugging arms spread wide wrapped around the skin of an animal I eat many weeknights the smallest hairs sprouting human-feeling
        from its skin

Begin in the name of [God]

Begin with Bahman Mohassess old man painter in his apartment in Italy in his [un]humble hermitage staring at a screen an ocean laughing pointing at his grave

—fine

Begin here Persian Picasso chain-smoking preaching sounds in the back of his throat to his desert body as he rises from his chair

Begin with [the living] the warm body

Bahman returning to Tehran destroying his masterworks laughing at the shorn canvas of their faces explaining how everything has a life [a death] and that these

these are [no] different

An animal dies while living, a human lives in death / the animal that is within me is dear to my heart

Begin [again]—*fine*
　　　　　and again in Persian

دوباره بگو
/begu dobāreh/
!again it say

Say it when you don't understand
　　　often I don't understand

Begin at the farm where lonely people are pimped out seventy-five dollars a hug to sullen cows hooves wrapped around where they wish to be

Begin Bahman buying colors in the streets of Italy—no sane artist buys gray they create gray

Begin muttering *Jesus Christ* at the neat murder of one praying mantis by another at the way life ends in the mouths of those closest to you

Keep the lonely things separate

Begin in the underwater wanting to end spread like [in] the ocean

Begin unsure of how I want to spread
        often I am unsure
        how do ashes spread [unsure] in the ocean

A worm has the right to crawl the earth, but I don't have that right

and the pigs are cute now will die soon when I was very young one peed in my arms on my jacket grandma snapped the picture look see if we just—

Bahman began dying in the middle of his own documentary spiting immortality

—begin with cow-arms wrapped around the lonely people smiling begin anywhere I, you

Begin

We were all of us afraid

They begin to wrap it up the Persian Picasso's life's work strung up like meats sell the paintings he promised he'd destroy color bleeding in all that cardboard

You need to learn to do this yourself

Begin now just [Persian] Picasso

Begin trudging back to the farm cottage on the hill near the singing brook settling up with the stars

So many fish spreading [swimming] in the green-blue

The other day a lightning bug sparked past my shoulder and out of instinct I swear it was [indistinct] I swatted it to the cement and
thought I killed it thought

Why did you do that you didn't [need to] do that

—fine

until it righted itself spread its wings reentered the garden and I wanted to shout

FIRST LOVE POEM

for Dad

I was always afraid of you. Your angry
grieving. Your stomping

around the house. And night moaning. And frightening
the dog. I was always afraid of

ruin. So that once I took a report card
and changed the fearful thing from D to B,

a dissection. Botched it, of course,
slashed a line through the heart of it

and decidedly stole into the nighttime storm lissome
as dirt. Treading back to the house,

spying on you, alone, working at
the dishes in the kitchen, your hands softening

in the stream. You were always so
compassionate. So when you interrupted

my 8 p.m. cartoons, your hair dripping
with the outside rain like Indiana Jones, I wondered

what it was you'd been trying to save. And when
you held my ink-streaked note to the sky,

asked *What is this?* I might have answered
it was my first love poem.

HERE'S A LOVE POEM TO THE GARDEN SNAIL

i can't remember anything from the moment
i was born until the moment they died. so
i write instead to the garden snail i once

poked and prodded in its box.
i could not have known or believed
in its treacherous lovemaking, in the

knotting of one thing to another,
in the death of anything. this snail, who,
in a boy's leisurely blink, disappeared

into the blackness of a tire's tread. it's as if
i never really existed. left by the roadside, clutching
myself to myself. can a person be a person

without memories? the car crashed. i
awoke, asking for my mother. nothing
is changed. i live, knowing they

died. tell me again how i
survived it. i was the clever hero. no, i
was the heavy-lidded driver. no, i

was the black-paved road. no, i
was the son. i closed my
eyes and fell out of the world, knowing

i'd fall back into it.

THE SEEN UNSEEN

Tubbrid Castle, Kilkenny, Ireland

Someone is always wishing to be in or out
       of these thin places. I've awoken
three times in this gloaming to a window
       blown off its hinges, three new spider bites
marching across Rachie's chest
       this morning. Dad sings to check the acoustics.
We booked this place because we only have
       one life. But now, I'm skeptical. Am I
afraid? The cows calling questions across
       one field to the next, the absence of
birds who made their nest a mile high in the stone
       masonry of my window, are a far cry
from the hauntings I'm used to. In the lack
       of mirror in my bathroom, I'm learning to self-
soothe. How did moving forward get to be
       through such abundance? So that my feet
slowed by the cold thrill of a fog-cloaked
       ocean, Dad's hands reaching for
my shoulders: many shoulders. Stubborn. In-
       satiable. Alive. Rachie snapping us into
stillness. What is a haunting? Anyway, I feel
       I could sleep here for ages.

SUSIE'S LETTER

October 27, 2001

My dear

Today   I wanted

                                        to celebrate.

You   oblivious!   Cyrus
                    the balloons
                            the candles,   he   kissed you.
                            I made   foolish mistakes.
photographs   no film

                                ghoulish

    . . . no photos   can't take photos when you're shooting blanks.
                    The other mistake

                            I should have known—the darn thing WAS
light   was empty! So I filled it up with
noise
Then   Cyrus.   You

                    your hands . . . and   and

the commotion of everyone around. And you

                                    And you   all over your   all
around your   even up your   We put you
                         everywhere.   you
looked   musical

                          opening

                          your morning breast   for anything. That
closeness   I hope I always

HOW LONG TO WAIT THERE WHEN THE BREATHING STOPS

Push the steaming chassis down the exit
ramp, walk two miles into the valley
for gasoline and a way to carry it. Loosening
our ties, scuffing our dress shoes. Joyful, thinking.

This is how it's always been, Dad and me
limping back from a funeral in the heat, knowing we
could take up residence in any of these roof-shorn
houses and try to fall asleep there. I've never known

how to wake him when he's being too loud
or too quiet. So still I want to hold my fingers to his
breathing. Body heat making his breath catch
fire, up his oxford button-down. A car gasping

aglow. Our luminous hearts. I'm singing and laughing.
My father is setting his jaw. When I look, he cracks a smile.

NOTES

The epigraph for this collection is from *Gold* by Rumi translated by the incredible Haleh Liza Gafori (New York Review Books, NYRB Classics, 2022).

"The Patient Stone" references the ongoing Women's Movement in Iran. I express my solidarity with the brave women of Iran and send prayers to all the families (mine included) who have been affected by the human rights atrocities committed by the Iranian government. I pray that we will soon find peace across the Middle East, and that one day, everyone will feel safe in their homes.

"Mother" is written after Susan Atefat-Peckham and Jean Valentine.

The bracketed language throughout the section "Book of Kin" is from the 2002 State of the Union Address, also known as the "Axis of Evil" Speech, given by then-President of the United States, George W. Bush. The italicized text that begins "Book of Kin" ("people are calling god with all their heart ..."), "Book of Sleep" ("many of us don't even believe in god ... "), and "Book of Dirt & Dust" ("defenseless people who have been called 'dirt and dust,' ...") is drawn from a YouTube video posted by Mehdi Saharkhiz, the son of a wrongfully incarcerated prisoner of the Islamic Republic of Iran, in the aftermath of the Green Movement protests.

"Haunt" is written for and after the poet, theologian, and women's rights activist Fatimah Baraghani, or Tāhirih, of the Bábí faith, who became a religious martyr after her death. She was executed in 1852 as a result of her public unveiling at the Conference of Badasht.

"Surroundings" is written in the form of a "Duplex" invented by Jericho Brown, a form that blends aspects of the sonnet and ghazal. Thank you, Jericho, for the way you subvert and honor and push forward tradition.

"Learning to Pray" borrows its title from a poem by Kaveh Akbar.

"Coronation" borrows from the traditions and rituals regarding ancestor worship described in the *Rites of Zhou* and is written after Ilya Kaminsky.

"Memorial Mural for the Persian [Picasso]" is written after Kazim Ali and takes inspiration from the documentary *Fifi Howls from Happiness* about the life and death of sculptor, painter, and poet, Bahman Mohassess. The italicized text beginning with *"An animal dies while living . . ."* and *"A worm has the right to crawl the earth . . ."* are the original compositions of Mr. Mohassess.

"Susie's Letter" is written in the form of an erasure of a letter written and addressed to me on my first birthday by my mother. While erasures can do many things to address (both public and private) grief, I'd like to note here that this poem's aims are to share and withhold, to be both generous and a bit selfish, to confront the pain inherent in surviving a beloved and also the joy of what survives of their lasting presence.

ACKNOWLEDGMENTS

Grateful acknowledgment is given to the editors of the journals and anthologies where early versions of these poems, sometimes with different titles and in different forms, first appeared:

Arkansas International: "Coronation" and "Sundered Sonnet: If We Should Be Ghosts"

Barrow Street: "In a Child's Hands"

Bellingham Review: "*dar havāyat*, in Your Air"

The Chattahoochee Review: "Imagine the Lake. Cyrus Is Alive"

Cutleaf: "Haunt," "Heathcliffs," "Once Mourned," and "The Patient Stone"

Diode: "Sundered Sonnet: They Say I Speak Better Persian Than"

The Florida Review: "I Learn a Language I'm Too Afraid to Speak"

Free State Review: "The Night before My Mother Died, They Slept in Separate Rooms"

The Georgia Review: "How Long to Wait There When the Breathing Stops," "The Turkish Coffee Lady," and "If I Want to Go There I Have to Watch What I Say"

The Harvard Advocate: "They Wake Me"

Interim: "Learning to Pray"

The Journal: "The House Where I Was Born"

Michigan Quarterly Review: "Second Mother"

Mizna: "Susie's Letter"

The Oxonian Review: "porthole" and "The Seen Unseen"

Peripheries: "Memorial Mural for the Persian [Picasso]"

Poetry: "Surroundings" and "Cyrus"

Qu: "First Love Poem"

Rattle: "All Bodies"

SOFTBLOW: "Of Blueberries"

Southeast Review: "here's a love poem sleeping"

Storm Cellar: "Wind Chimes"
Tinderbox Poetry Journal: "here's a love poem to the garden snail"
Tupelo Quarterly: "Post-loss Checklist"

"Of Blueberries" and "Wind Chimes" won the 2020 Breakout 8 Writers Prize for Poetry selected by judge Marcus Wicker and were reprinted in *Epiphany*.

"Second Mother" (originally titled "This Happens") reappeared in *Poetry Daily*.

"I Learn a Language I'm Too Afraid to Speak," received a special mention in the 2023 Pushcart Prize Anthology, *Pushcart Prize XLVII: Best of the Small Presses*.

Many of these poems also appeared in the limited edition chapbook *How Many Love Poems* (Seven Kitchens Press, 2021).

Oceans of love and gratitude to all my teachers and mentors at Interlochen Arts Academy, Harvard University, and The Michener Center for Writers at UT-Austin, especially Brittany Cavallaro, Josh Bell, Jorie Graham, Tracy K. Smith, and Joanna Klink, all of whom worked closely with me on these poems, treated my story with tenderness, taught me to love poetry and the written word, and set an example of care for me to follow. Thank you to January Gill O'Neil, Tracy K. Smith, Naomi Shihab Nye, and Mark Doty for the light of your work and your words, and gifting them in support of this book. I'm star-struck and astounded and grateful.

Thank you to everyone at Autumn House Press, especially Mike Good, Christine Stroud, and Melissa Dias-Mandoly for being so patient and kind in the face of my many anxieties, and for being such attentive shepherds of this work as it makes its way into the world.

Thank you to Hemad Javadzade for allowing us to use his beautiful piece *The Now* as the cover art of this book.

Thank you to my beloveds in words and music, especially Athena Nassar, Yanna Cassell, Sophie Paquette, Cookie Dutch, Helena Notario, Bryson Parker, Tawanda Mulalu, Kailani Michiko Biehl, Sunny Butterfield, Siavash Saadlou, Sherah Bloor, Emma De Lisle, Harry Hall, Sam Bailey, Katherine Irajpanah, Vanessa Braganza, Marie Ungar, Lana Reeves, Brammy Rajakumar,

Benjamin Ballet, Carissa Chen, Elaine Kim, Ava Salzman, Ben Lee, Cade Williams, Alex Braslavsky, Mercedes Rodriguez, Kinsale Drake, Isabel Duarte-Gray, and Timothy Ashley Leo, for your inspiration, mentorship, love, and many kindnesses. I'm so lucky.

Oceans of love and gratitude to Isabella Farmer. When I think of song, of who I'm writing with and toward, you're who I see. Thank you for your music, your kindness, your adventurous spirit, your silliness, and your unending belief in me.

Thank you to all my beloveds in Huntington, West Virginia, who were always so supportive of my writing, even when it meant it would take me away from home. Thank you for gifting me such a beautiful childhood and young adulthood.

Oceans and oceans of love and gratitude to my parents, Joel and Rachael Peckham, who taught me all the many ways we can connect in poetry, who read with me every night at (a way too early) bedtime and instilled in me a love for the written word. Your love inspires me every day. I want to be just like you. Thank you for taking such good care of me. Thank you for being my home.

Oceans of love and gratitude to all my grandparents, Papa and Bibi, Joel and Jeanne, and Mike and Diane, for being my biggest supporters, and for loving me so unconditionally. You are my first teachers, my best storytellers, and an endless source of inspiration. You are dear to me.

Oceans of love and prayer for all my ancestors, especially Susan Atefat-Peckham, Cyrus Atefat-Peckham, Joel Peckham Sr., Nina Barati, Esmat Sharifian Barati, Hasan Barati, and Muhammad Atefat. Wherever you are, I hope you are together there. This book is for you.

Endless love and gratitude to all my extended family, especially The Kemps, The Maidments, The Woodruffs, The Pridgeons, and The Huyser-Pridgeons, and to all my cousins, Anna, Brandon, Claire, Eric, Natalie, Drew, Tatum, Owen, Mac, and Declan, who never place any limitations on our closeness, and who treat me like a sibling when I need it most. I love you all so much.

Oceans of gratitude to my Iranian family, who speak to me on the phone in Persian, whose unconditional love and passion surrounds and astounds me, especially Lili, Ezat, Sheida, Sholeh, Mustafa, and Siamak. I delight in your presence. I promise I will visit someday.

I wouldn't succeed in naming everyone who had a hand in my upbringing, who treated me like their own family in the wake of the accident, who never asked for apology or thanks, and who helped me reconceptualize what it means to be kin—spiritually, artistically, and living here on this earth, together. I could never exhaust that list of names, that catalog of gratitude, that book of kin. For that, and for now, to all my beloveds: Thank you.

NEW AND FORTHCOMING FROM AUTUMN HOUSE PRESS

Book of Kin by Darius Atefat-Peckham

Winner of the 2023 Autumn House Poetry Prize , selected by January Gill O'Neil

Near Strangers by Marian Crotty

Winner of the 2023 Autumn House Fiction Prize, selected by Pam Houston

Deep & Wild: On Mountains, Opossums & Finding Your Way in West Virginia
by Laura Jackson

Winner of the 2023 Autumn House Nonfiction Prize, selected by Jenny Boully

Terminal Maladies by Okwudili Nebeolisa

Winner of the 2023 CAAPP Book Prize, selected by Nicole Sealey

I Have Not Considered Consequences: Short Stories by Sherrie Flick

The Worried Well by Anthony Immergluck

Winner of the 2024 Rising Writer Prize, selected by Eduardo C. Corral

Rodeo by Sunni Brown Wilkinson

Winner of the 2024 Donald Justice Poetry Prize, selected by Patricia Smith

For our full catalog please visit: http://www.autumnhouse.org